# PIER 40

*A Poetic Story by*

# Joyce Englander Levy

*Finishing Line Press*
Georgetown, Kentucky

# PIER 40

Publisher: Leah Huete de Maines
Editor: Christen Kincaid
Cover Art: Katherine Kane
Author Photo: Gort Productions, Alex Gort
Cover Design: Elizabeth Maines McCleavy


Order online: www.finishinglinepress.com
also available on amazon.com

Author inquiries and mail orders:
Finishing Line Press
PO Box 1626
Georgetown, Kentucky 40324
USA

# Contents

*dedicated to*
*Laurie Englander*

## OUTSIDE

We're walking west across Twelfth Street towards
the Hudson River. I'm with my children, Vaughn
and Nikola, on a feisty August afternoon. It's 2020.

The kids run their hands along brick walls
and metal banisters; I don't ask them
to stop touching everything. Vigilance becomes depleting.

During the first few months of the pandemic,
the kids broke the swivel chairs from spinning so hard;
my husband, Ariel, set up his desk at the counter—

not realizing he would sit on a metal bar stool for months;
I closed our bedroom door and led daily meditations
on social media, while Ariel researched PPP loans

and helped our kids sign-in for twenty-minutes of *school*.
By July, we were ready for space, so when
the Downtown United Soccer Club

announced a socially distanced camp, we signed up.
That's where we're headed.
"Mommy, I'm thirsty," Niko says, pulling on my hand.

We pause for a drink of water in front of Café Cluny.
I peer inside the bistro and remember—
clinks of glasses, herb omelets, salty fries.

I see where I leaned in on wooden tables
to listen closely.
So many entrepreneurial friends I have met here.

The pleasure of seeing each other included
the pleasure of getting ready to be together.
I can still hear my friends:

*I keep the big picture in mind.*
*I know my strengths and I know my limits.*
*I believe in you, write it down.*

*I like to be in control, so does he.*
*I'm on my luteal phase.*
*Let yourself be lucky, but if there's luck there's chance.*

I put the boys' water bottles in my bag. They pretend
they're on a carousel and walk around me in circles.
This is one of those cobblestone intersections

that simultaneously defines a neighborhood
and transports you to an earlier era. Four city blocks
can be paved with asphalt in a single day,

or a mere two hundred square feet of cobbles
can be laid in the same space of time.
I advocate for the slow roads.

That's partially why
I recently resigned
from a job I loved.

Before the pandemic,
I wanted motherhood to be paved;
I tried to cover ground smoothly and productively.

Now, I am on my knees laying bricks.
I leave time to play, to disagree, to explore.
But, even after years of studying non-violence

and how to create a life of inquiry over output,
I still yearn for productivity and efficiency.
Alas, I look at my phone, "Come on guys, time to go."

# TREASURE

I relax my eyes to gaze ahead.
What do I see in the tree-lined streets?
This is a day of abundance,

a day to leave behind
a small treasure
for someone to find.

What I do not see: other pedestrians. No sounds
of jackhammering, no loose smells of urine, no tourists
walking by with a bounce in their step speaking Italian.

Niko places his hand in mine. We wait to cross Eighth Avenue.
I look back and see Vaughn jump-kick off a brick wall
in a one-eighty. He's just like his father,

who still points out rails he skated on as a kid. I want
to ask Vaughn to stop,
but instead I direct my desire for calm

to myself, not him.
Calm doesn't yet come naturally to me.
I crave it, but

I am sensitive and excitable.
Calm is
something I strive for. Maybe that's the problem.

I started practicing yoga and meditation when
I was seventeen. My antidote. I immersed myself
in the yoga world; it felt safe to be with people who

were deliberately cleansing their nerve endings.
I've taught yoga and managed studios for decades.
I even co-founded a studio in the Flatiron District.

However, by restricting my lifestyle as much as I did,
I didn't learn to integrate my practices into family life.
It took lockdown to finally acknowledge this.

I could decently manage work stress, kind of,
if my family life was easy going enough,
but I was not so skillful at managing home stressors.

I evaded chaos
by evanescing to work and guaranteeing
more from myself in every meeting.

Prior to the pandemic, I was the head of mindful movement
at an integrative health and wellness start-up, where
I was invited to join a team of western doctors

and holistic practitioners, to share ideas and collaborate
on custom programming that would address
modern health concerns from multiple vantages.

No one perspective was considered the best.
Collaboration was built on mutual respect and curiosity.
I experienced my role as a joyful but serious responsibility.

The most important part was deciding who to recruit.
I helped the company grow to over a hundred employees
in the first year. It was a lot.

Thankfully, the founders aspired to create a culture
of wellness for our team. They supported me in leaving early
on Wednesdays to take the boys to piano lessons,

but otherwise I rarely made it home for dinner because
I liked creating in the office, and because
my children ate dinner before five o'clock.

So even prior to the pandemic—
I found my children's schedules did not align
with my schedule as an adult.

We opened the wellness center
a few months before lockdown.
Then everything changed.

After preparing for an in-person offering
we had the capability to help people,
we just had to rework our business model.

I was eager to try.
I didn't foresee how drastically my career
and my parenthood would collide.

# TRANSITIONS

I used to think shuttling the kids from place to place
was merely in-between time,
but then I learned these walks are main events.

They carry potent opportunities for connection
like a backpack on a day's shoulder.
We cross the street.

Niko starts singing, "What a Wonderful World".
The boys inch across a rope of fencing as we cut through
Abington Square: a romantic little park

where I once had a first kiss.
A trio of pigeons flap away. The city is hot.
I select from the perimeter of benches—flowers all around.

I take out my phone: no messages. I video the boys
sword fighting, and then I turn the camera around
and I'm somehow surprised to see myself.

I'm wearing a mask. My hair looks flat and needs a trim,
my green eyes look tired, my skin is pale, I need to tweeze,
and there is that lightning-bolt furrow etched between my brows.

I'm being hard on myself, I know. I tousle my hair,
massage my forehead, adjust my necklace,
and I put the phone down without taking a selfie because

who cares? I both do and don't miss feeling important.
It took twenty years to hike up my professional mountain.
It took one phone call to resign.

I hear a bird call.
I look up to see four bluejays on a branch.
For all that is gone, the city is still spawning surprises.

## BOUND

The last day our office was open,
my friend and I walked home together.
We stopped on Fifth Avenue. The city felt eerie.

The apocalyptic sensation was familiar from movies
but not life. I had seasonal allergies; I knew they
were allergies, but I still feared I was infected.

Infected: that word lived up to its potential.
Part of me feared this was really the end, like The End,
like if anyone survived, they would live in hazmat suits.

Part of me feared it was the end in smaller ways,
like the end of the start-up we had worked so hard to open.
The city wasn't vacant yet, like it would become;

it had a frantic energy of unclear deadlines.
I can't remember if my friend and I hugged goodbye.
That would have been scary, but knowing us, we did.

The time-lapse speed of letting go had begun.
Letting go of people. Letting go of routines.
Letting go of security. Letting go of dreams.

Letting go of freedoms and familiar scenes.
That evening, one of the founders called
to ask if I could lead daily meditations on social.

At that point I knew my children's schools were closed,
but I agreed to broadcast from my home
which gave me reason to get ready every morning.

The best thing about teaching meditation
(compared to parenting)
is that people listen to me.

My kids love negotiating,
and their job is *not* to do *everything* I say.
But when people showed up for yoga,

they appreciated the detail I described subtle sensations in,
and my precise adjustments to access breath in new ways.
I'm grateful I had the chance to teach in the pandemic.

The aspect of yoga I respect the most is simply:
students showing up.
So when people came to class, I felt in awe.

The live experience created familiar connections of community,
and it was my only sure break from parenting.
The rest of the day I was interruptible.

As it became evident the city would not re-open,
we erected a plan to move my department online.
This felt exciting and daunting.

If we succeeded, we could keep teachers employed
and provide for students.
We created a complimentary membership for first responders

who came to class after long shifts in the ER.
We wanted to help.
I tried.

To make schedules, I considered what people's days were like,
and when they might be free for classes. Thinking that way
highlighted how unpredictable the world had become.

I am perspiring sitting in the shade. I notice the metallic odor
of my sweat, like it smells when I'm worried. The breeze
is a maternal reminder to enjoy the passing day.

## UPHOLDING

"Are you hungry? Do you want a banana?" I ask.
Niko pulls down his mask and takes small bites.
Vaughn's mask is already down; he eats the whole

banana in two chews and climbs in my lap. "Mommy,
if all the animals in all the world would roar at the
same time—that's how loud my love is."

Then he ROARS in my ear, hops up, takes out his ball,
and dribbles around the path. I feel a pressure
to uphold so much. I stare into the blue sky.

During the beginning of the pandemic, personalities
ricocheted around our home in random bursts.
Vaughn needed constant movement.

Ariel held loud calls in the middle of the living room.
Niko gave up his afternoon nap. I couldn't
keep up with all the feeding, bathing, cleaning, soothing.

I always felt I was letting someone down, except
when I led meditations. When I tried to do other work
my children needed me and vice versa.

I want to be attentive to who I am with. I built
my career on the philosophical importance of doing so.
What happened when too many people needed me at once

wasn't pretty. My husband was equally overwhelmed,
fulfilling obligations to his extended family.
Neither one of us had extra to offer.

At one point Ariel said, "Maybe I married the wrong woman."
Yeah, well, maybe I married the wrong man.
We were in a fierce competition for free time.

A different family could have pulled it all off. Many did.
I thought hard about what Ariel said versus what he meant.
Something had to give. I resented the assumption

it should be my career. Resigning would be giving up
part of my identity. I feared not having income.
I feared being judged for quitting, and what this shift would do

to our marriage in the long run and to my friendships.
But not just for the sake of my marriage,
also for my own integrity, I disassembled my life.

"Here," Niko drops his banana peel in my lap,
and he runs off to join his brother. It would be so much easier
to throw it away myself. I call him back.

It's humiliating, but in July, I felt I was short-circuiting.
The pace at work was too fast,
and the children's pace was too immediate.

I was building Legos with Niko, reading global health reports,
researching breathing techniques, and helping Vaughn
with writing assignments on a new technology.

When the pandemic struck,
I began living in a company-wide Zoom meeting
where I was in my kitchen massaging kale with olive oil

and agreeing to do an interview with Coverture about
how meditation can help more than ever right now,
but then muting so I could yell at my kids to stop screaming.

A balance of parenthood and career
was not all I wanted to figure out.
It was my deep need to cultivate peace,

and my sense that—
I had no right to speak of it professionally
until I solved for it at home.

## NEVER SAY ALWAYS

We cross Washington Street and Vaughn says,
"Motorcycles! Three…two…one… It's a go!"
"Fly drive!" Niko yells.

This is a game they invented.
Vaughn pretends his hand is a motorcycle,
and Niko shouts commands as fast as he can.

They use the actual landscape
to create an alternate reality with
true emotion infused into the play.

"Big jump! Hover! No! I said, hover!" Niko says.
"Wah, wah. Game over," Vaughn teases.
I have no idea how to play, but it's clear

that Vaughn wants to be in charge. I stoop down.
"Buddy, is it possible for Niko to win?
Being competitive doesn't mean you always win,"

"Exactly," Vaughn says.
Well, that backfired.
"I never win. Never!" Niko says.

I look at them and see Niko, age three,
and Vaughn, age six, trying to make sense of
how they feel, and what they want, and what to do.

"I know it can feel that way, sweetheart, I do."
I do. A few weeks ago, I spent the morning on the
phone with my team of teachers while performing a

silent puppet show for the kids. On the one hand,
I was doing my job and building a new schedule—
in my other hand was a stuffed animal named Roy

who was pretending to be on the phone and making fun of me.
The teachers I spoke with were understanding and grateful.
They also had good ideas to share.

The kids were laughing and grasping at me.
I was dizzy.
That had been a tough week.

I wanted to surrender to the creative needs of my company.
But I am a teacher by nature, and my children
were no longer learning how to read.

Vaughn's teacher was camera shy,
so he would do a quick read-aloud
and then abruptly end class.

Niko's preschool recorded teachers singing songs, and then
laid most of the teachers off, so our son was expected to watch
videos of his former teachers maintaining old morning routines

for a mere twenty-minutes each morning.
Needless to say—my kids needed me.
I thought there was a solution in sight:

once I wrapped on establishing a new schedule,
I wouldn't have to make several hour-long calls every day,
and the new online curriculum would be settled

so I could simply manage it, and give my kids some attention,
and maybe I could get more than three-hours of sleep at night.
I was used to being sleep deprived, but this new low

was another reason alarms were sounding in my brain.
Perhaps because I have owned my own business,
and because stakes felt so high,

it never occurred to me to take a day off.
By the time I settled the schedule,
the CDC had changed guidelines,

the city's policies shifted, who remembers what else?
But everything needed to be reconsidered,
and I couldn't.

Another week of time-consuming scheduling
would mean another week we were all stuck on screens.
Then more complicated circumstances emerged.

My father became seriously ill. He survived Covid,
but was diagnosed with diabetes and he was hospitalized.
No visitors.

Also, I was living near Fifth Avenue, which meant
I was living in the heart of major protests
after George Floyd's death.

Vaughn began learning about racism in his read-alouds
and he had questions.
We took the boys to protests in the park.

At night there were fires, screams, sirens, and shouts
in a chorus of poignant high and low pitches
I will never forget.

I was both in the protests and insulated from them.
I wanted racism to crumble. I wanted mutual respect to thrive.
I wanted to practice right effort in this hard moment.

I examined myself. I had tough conversations.
I vowed to do what I could to grow,
and first and foremost, to respond to people with care.

## SECRET HANDSHAKE

Niko's understandably upset about *Motorcycles*.
Vaughn's concerned. We're on Washington Street
near a yellow brick courtyard landscaped with hydrangeas.

I am stooped down low, looking between them. I say,
"You know what, guys? This stuff isn't easy.
You're both little boys who are learning,

and I'm a mommy who's learning. But one thing I know—
it doesn't feel good when it's impossible to succeed.
We need to believe we have a chance,

and that the people we love are rooting for us.
Is there a way for you two to play this game
that is more fun for both of you?"

Vaughn turns to Niko and says,
"Do you want to download a new command?"
Niko says, "Yes! How do I get it?"

"By not whining."
"Okay," Niko says as seriously as he can.
"You two are good at figuring things out," I say.

I turn around so they can do their secret handshake,
and they are back to being friendly conspirators.
We make it to the final block before the water.

We hang back several feet from the curb as six columns
of sparse West Side Highway traffic speeds by.
"Hold my hand," I say over the cars.

## DIVIDED

Before I resigned, I asked myself,
How many responsibilities can I divide life by
and feel whole?

Innately, I needed to be true
to my American dream upbringing, as well as
my less-is-more moral compass.

In my twenties, I supported people, mostly women and mothers,
to develop their ability to care for themselves,
but part of my message was,

*The better we care for ourselves, the better we can care for others.*
By my mid-thirties, I was caring for people
professionally and personally. I needed support,

but I no longer knew what kind or where it should be
coming from. It became hard to prioritize my career when
my income essentially covered the cost of childcare.

It was hard to model resilience when I felt chronically rushed.
It was always quicker to tie my children's shoes for them.
I couldn't preach principles of mindfulness

when my peace was dangling by a thread.
My arms held more yes's than they could carry.
My young children want me to look with all my senses.

They want to eat, if I put the food in their mouth.
They want to play, if I sit on the floor and build blocks too.
When I resigned,

the kids and I took the red stop sign,
made out of construction paper,
off my door and we ripped it up.

Being home with my children every day, I fully realized
what I had been missing. Their sounds,
which quickly morphed from cooing to giggling,

to whining, yelling, crying—their young, high-pitched
noises sounded so—temporary. However,
resigning didn't mean my ambitions suddenly vanished.

I grew up wanting a career. When I was young, I played
by putting on my mom's heels. I called myself Christy,
and I was the boss.

Or I stood in front of a class of stuffed animal students
and I taught them what I learned in school from the alphabet
to algebra to conjugating verbs in French.

Ideally, my husband and I both wanted careers,
and to be involved, creative parents. In reality,
we both grew up in old-fashioned homes.

Our dads ran family businesses. Our moms ran our houses.
If my husband made breakfast, then he was doing more
than what had been modeled for him.

If I had a nanny (before the pandemic),
then I was doing far less than my mom did at home.
I've spoken with mothers who are breadwinners,

and others from countries and cultures
with more progressive systems.
They don't harbor the same guilt I do.

The guilt: when there was a family morning,
and I had to decide between speaking on a panel
or helping my son's class with their art project.

When I could meet a VP about a brand partnership,
or watch my child sing in the spring concert.
When the school called to inform us Vaughn needed glasses,

and the doctor chastised Ariel for not bringing him sooner,
and Ariel blamed me, because he had noticed
Vaughn couldn't read the Knicks scores on the tv,

so I had taken him to the pediatrician, but apparently
that wasn't sufficient, and I wasn't there for my son
when he learned his right eye may go blind,

because I was working with the sports medicine team
learning to evaluate students' potential for injury.
And the shame—when I talked to my friends

who were stay at home moms, I felt ashamed
for missing PTA meetings and pick-ups.
When I talked to friends who worked outside the home,

I felt ashamed for not being further in my career.
When I talked to my mother-in-law I felt ashamed
for not having shabbat dinner ready earlier,

and not doing more to provide cultural ties for my children.
I don't have only one culture to teach them.
I grew up Episcopalian. I study Yoga and Buddhism.

My husband's family is Jewish, and the most important
thing to them is bringing the family together
and celebrating friends as family.

One moment I felt stuck as my colleagues raced past me.
The next moment I was rushing from my children,
who were begging me not to go.

But, at the end of the day, I never missed a bedtime.
I would sit next to them, both of their beds side by side,
so I could scratch their backs.

# MOVING ON

"Five! Four! Three!" the kids shout. We make it
across the West Side Highway. The kids run to the
Hudson River. It must be high tide; I hear waves hitting

the bulkhead. We walk downtown. My generation
of female friends was encouraged to have careers,
and my parents consistently told me I could do anything I wanted,

but an undercurrent eroded the foundation under my ambitions,
perhaps because I was also taught to find intrinsic value
for my work rather than to work for compensation.

Starting when I was ten, I babysat my sister, typically for free.
We would play dolls or brush each other's hair on Friday
nights. In high school, beyond chores like vacuuming,

I grocery shopped and often cooked dinner.
I took charge and prepared healthy meals.
I earned mostly A's, but

when I asked if,
like my friends,
I might be paid

for good grades,
my parents told me, "No.
Work for the sake of learning, not to earn money."

I'm not saying parents must pay kids for good grades.
But I'm trying to understand why I was being raised
to be both a hard worker, and

someone who shouldn't expect to be
compensated for her work.
No one taught me about money—

not how to invest nor how to plan a financial future.
That wasn't part of having a life
I was expected to be in charge of.

Maybe I missed the lessons. Maybe my parents expected
my future husband to be in charge. Maybe they didn't know.
I am the first woman in my family to graduate from college.

It often feels like a career is self-indulgent relative to
the life of my foremothers: homemakers who sacrificed
for family and expected daughters to do the same.

# A MEMORY

I was sitting cross-legged, studying for an AP Bio exam,
and my mom called me downstairs.
Reluctantly, I left my notecards in a pile on the floor.

My mom wanted me to unload the dishwasher.
"But I'm studying," I said.
"My test could count for college credit."

"Joycie, I need help."
My mom kept a spotless house.
She took care of everything and everyone,

including my grandfather, who lived with us.
She had wanted to go to college,
but she went straight to work after

being the president of her high school's work-study program.
She started her career at Ohio Bell in the 1970's,
and after long days of supporting dispatchers,

she drove, over an hour, to night classes at a local university.
She was promoted to a management program. Then,
she married her high school sweetheart, my dad, after he

graduated from college. Before she could graduate,
they started our family.
To support his career and to be there for my siblings and I,

she resigned and became a stay-at-home mom.
There was a lot of love, and a lot of resentment
that burst free in greater frequency as time went on.

My grandmother leaned on my mother, her oldest daughter,
heavily, to sustain their house and care for her four younger
siblings. My mom, in turn, wanted more help from me—

her oldest daughter—more than I was willing to give.
I wanted to study; I refused to unload the dishwasher.
I ended up grounded, and I still had to put dishes away.

Now, I wonder what else was happening for my mom that day.
Mothers need help. It's complicated to raise a child
who spends hours doing schoolwork while

there is plenty of housework to be shared.
Perhaps, if I had unloaded the dishwasher
and returned to studying, I would have learned

the balance I struggle with. I can hear my mom
cheering at that reconciliation. Yet, I know I was fighting
for something that wasn't being understood in my home.

I can't imagine forcing my sons
to unload the dishwasher before a big exam.
What was valued in my upbringing?

I valued school and I wanted a career;
my parents were trying to teach me to balance
my ambitions with caring for family.

# GENERATIONS

I was born in 1981. That's the first year of Gen Y.
I was among the first of my millennial friends
to come to the parent-career crossroads.

I was raised in a pre-social media time and shown
through shows like Full House and Growing Pains
that a home doesn't need to be run by a mom.

I was also taught—by many stay-at-home-moms
in my community who perhaps transferred
their unactualized ambitions to us girls—

marriage and motherhood may not lead to happiness.
Those moms wanted more for me,
yet I was still being prepared for the work of caregiving,

which I was expected to grow into. I witnessed mothers
take pride in, and become overwhelmed by,
caring for their families—

from kids and husbands, to ailing in-laws,
to troubled siblings—which often, somehow,
resulted in their loneliness.

I thought the solution was
to NOT give up my well-being
for the sake of others.

But now here I am reconciling the deluge of family needs—
from people who need care and whom I care deeply about.
I was losing hair over raising two Gen Alpha boys,

and beginning to care for Boomer parents,
while trying to keep up with my health
in a career in which appearance often determines credibility.

## IT'S LATE AFTERNOON

The summer sun is high and heading west over the Hudson.
Light is coming at an angle. We walk along the river,
past the bronze apple sculpture and bees pollinating begonias.

The boys jump over long shadows cast by young trees,
wooden benches, and a few people as we pass. The boys
lose or gain points when they do or don't land on a shadow.

I marvel at how they come up with these games. We stop
to throw pennies into the river. The water looks like tarnished
silver, and our wishes penetrate through the lively surface.

The boys take sidewalk chalk from my bag.
They trace shadows:
one of the treasures we'll leave behind today.

## FAMILY VALUES

"I don't think I'll get married or have kids,"
I once told my brother. He replied, "What are you talking about?
You are definitely the kind of girl who will."

I almost didn't to prove him wrong.
I did (partially) because of his confidence in who I was.
I've made sacrifices to commit to and build my family.

But that's life.
I'm deeply grateful for my husband and kids.
What I'm grappling with is what this means

within a system that depends on
trillions of dollars in unpaid labor from intelligent,
caring, capable people (mostly women) in the name of

love. The love is real, and motivating, and many people
are grateful for the intimacy and purpose inherent in the work
and so they're willing to do it for free,

but at the same time, we could come up with
a more worldly system. For it isn't just
moms who miss out as a result of these imbalances.

## RENOVATIONS TAKE TIME

Here I am, peering at forty and going through
what some might call a midlife crisis—but
I'm referring to it as an identity renovation.

I want to implore women to NOT give up on their careers,
and I want to suggest the real risks in doing so.
Yet, I resigned. I created a solution in the pandemic,

because families with young children in America often
have few good options. Something must give—
whether personally or professionally.

By the time there might be solutions—
like employee benefits that include more time given
for family and personal life—

like nationwide, affordable, state-of-the-art childcare
centers staffed with well-educated, well-paid, caregivers—
like workdays that coincide with schooldays—

By then, my kids will be grown,
and I'll wish I had more time with them.
And so, cycles continue.

## WATERFRONT PARK

I watch a family of geese: their speckled brown feathers,
long black necks, webbed feet,
and the cautious distance they keep from us.

I look past the Hudson River estuary and see weathered wooden
columns of a pier long gone. I look further south and see
the distant steadfast Statue of Liberty.

I think of my ancestors who came here from Austria,
Ireland, France, and I wonder if any of them left
treasured wishes here on Manhattan's shore.

"Okay. Pack it up. Let's hustle, kiddos," I say.
Niko says, "Fine, but can you hold me?
Hold me! Hold me, Mommy!"

"Okay, for a minute." I lift Nikola. His limbs
wrap around me. His plump cheek presses to mine.
Holding him uplifts me too, for a moment,

but then his weight settles. It's like holding
a bag of water the way his body fits against mine.
"I need to put you down, buddy."

"No!" he says and wraps tighter around me.
I squeeze him closer and say,
"Oh no, I forgot to tell you, I put on the super glue."

At this, he claims unsticking power, and he slides down
me like I'm a firepole. He sits on my feet. Vaughn sits on a bench,
crosses his arms, pretends to relax, then pops up and

runs to the next seat. The kids were in school one day,
then completely isolated the next and suddenly running
into *No's* every six feet. I needed to find opportunities

for them to feel free and safe. Now I'm available to help them
get along, to answer their questions about how they could spend
a dollar, or to discuss who Ruby Bridges is.

Vaughn asks, "Mommy,
what were you like when you were young?"
"I was a lot more spontaneous," I say.

"Mommy, would you rather sit in horrible traffic
one day and zero traffic the next day,
or so-so traffic every day?"

"How about we walk where we need to go?"
"No. You have to choose."
They love making me choose.

We approach the three story, rusty, blue and white building
that forms the exterior of our destination.
The boys slide their hands along metal and wood railings

that keeps them from falling into the river.
"Guys, please stop touching *everything*."
I sanitize their hands, and we're all annoyed with me.

# FINALLY

Pier 40. Where a rectangle of AstroTurf hides
like a portal of green freedom inside a multi-level,
musty parking lot. To a downtown kid this place,

which only the organized can score a permit for,
is relief. The kids run to catch a friend.
This is the farthest I've been from them in days.

A truth in me persists, a truth I'm trying to understand.
It's a truth that feels like a secret. But it isn't a secret;
it merely feels like one because I don't understand it.

It's like part of me that developed in girlhood is standing
at a juncture that joins four of my interior corridors:
Contentment, Ambition, Resentment, and Gratitude.

It occurs to me, what feels like a secret is this question:
*What if making space for my children is also my chance
to circle back to a path I wanted to be on years ago?*

I want to finally prioritize a dream,
which I've kept in my life like a nearly-dead orchid.
I want to be here for my kids now, and

to slowly cultivate purpose outside my home.
I want to value my work as a mother
and to live in a society which values what I learn.

"Guys, wait, come here," I call.
I kneel to tie their shoelaces into double knots.
I slip shin guards into their socks, and I watch them run off.

I sneak inside the fence, but outside the field
to pull out my notebook
and write.

## SELF-REGULATION

A reliable blue and white sky; a map.
Is this a cloud's day off or prime time?
If a cloud is a could, could the sky be the why?

Be content. Clouds cannot be late. Why worry about
momentum? The clouds are moving along, barely—
A secret ballet. Applause of ocean.

Taste of communal thirst.
If only someone could reach down
and remind me

I'm loved.
Better appreciate
days like these.

Days that conjure slow
seductive tones
as if to inquire

casually,
ready to go?
Voices calling out from the ground

sound small in the distance.
Clouds separate, drift, unite,
change shape—with traceable slowness.

## TREASURE

I tear out the page, fold up the paper,
and I hide the poem beneath the bench
for someone to find. We're in this together.

I look up to see my son running toward me.
"Mommy, did you see that?"
"I'm sorry, Buddy, what did I miss?"

"That cloud looked like a penguin!"
Then he drops his water bottle on the ground
in front of me, and he runs back onto the field.

# Self · Regulation

A reliable blue
and white sky; a map.
Is this a cloud's
day off
or prime time?
If a cloud
is a cold
Could the sky
be the why?
Be content.
Clouds cannot
be late.
                Why

Worry about
momentum?
The clouds are
moving along,
barely —
A secret ballet.
Applause of ocean.
Taste of communal
thirst. If only
        Someone

Could
reach down
and remind me
I'm loved.
Better appreciate
days like these.
Days that
Conjure slow
Seductive tones
as if to inquire
Casually
        ready to go?


Voices
Calling out
from the ground
Sound small
in the distance.
Clouds seperate,
drift, unite,
change shape
with traceable
    slowness.
        Joyce E. Levy

31

## WITH SPECIAL THANKS

To my sons, my suns, my stars—Vaughn and Nikola Levy.

To my poetry teacher, Genine Lentine, for her literary wisdom. When I first read her "Self-Regulation" she asked me what led up to the poem. I told her about this walk. Genine wrote down my words, sent them to me, and encouraged me to keep writing this story.

To the Creative Writing department at Florida International University, especially Les Standiford and Julie Marie Wade.

To Katherine Kane for her artistry. After she read the manuscript, she had the idea for utilizing the cobblestone pattern in the cover art. I sent her a few photos from in front of Café Cluny. K Kane created the pattern and layered it in with a map of the walk towards Pier 40.

To Michele Herman for teaching me to write memoir. After reading my manuscript, she pushed me to clarify and be more specific in the areas I was reluctant and holding back.

To Finishing Line Press for taking a chance on me. I entered a contest for Emerging Women's Voices in 2023. I didn't win the contest, but they accepted my submission to publish *Pier 40* in their general collection.

To my first readers for keeping me honest: My Narrative Healing Listening Circle, Emily Gerard, Jules Ferree Tesoriero, Ariel Levy, Vaughn Levy, Nikola Levy, Rebecca Parekh, Joanna Englander, Laurie Englander.

To my husband, family, friends, students, and confidants for their encouragement and support.

To you, dear reader.

**Joyce Englander Levy** is a mother, writer, and poet, and she has taught yoga and meditation for over twenty years. She graduated Cum Laude from Miami University in 2003 with degrees in Psychology and Linguistics with a minor in Poetry. While in university, she did research in the field of Positive Psychology. She collaborated with the Dean of Student Affairs to create leadership programming for the university, and she completed her first (of many) yoga teacher trainings. Joyce went on to teach at and manage yoga studios in Chicago, Montauk, and New York City. She was a co-founder of Yoga Shanti NYC, and she established the mindful movement program for an integrative health and wellness company called, The Well. Joyce has continued to study poetry and writing in Yale's Writers' Workshops, in classes at The Writer's Studio, and with weekly mentorship from Genine Lentine. Joyce currently lives in Miami, Florida where she is working towards her M.F.A. in Creative Writing at Florida International University; she publishes a substack called *Look Both Ways*, which explores relationships between creativity and meditation; and she is a volunteer reader for Only Poems. *Pier 40* is her first published chapbook.

www.ingramcontent.com/pod-product-compliance
Lightning Source LLC
Chambersburg PA
CBHW022045080426

42734CB00009B/1238